GOD'S INDWELLING

SPIRIT

Thanks for your dedicate life and service in evangelism and missions. May the Lord bless you both. Thanks for hosting us in Singapore.

Furman

By
F. Furman Kearley, Ph. D.
Chairman, Biblical Studies Division
Lubbock Christian College

ISBN 0-88428-035-7

PARCHMENT PRESS
P. O. Box 3909
Birmingham, Alabama 35208

i

This edition has been published especially for Alabama Christian College and may be ordered from the college bookstore at 5345 Atlanta Highway, Montgomery, Ala. 36109.

FOREWORD

The Lectureship at Alabama Christian College in the Spring of 1974 was one of the best ever conducted on this campus. The crowds were great, interest was high and many great speeches were made.

Dr. F. Furman Kearley, Head of the Bible Department at Lubbock Christian College, spoke on the subject, "God's Indwelling Spirit." In recent years much has been written and spoken on this important subject. The material in this booklet will convince the reader that Dr. Kearley has given much study and thought to God's indwelling Spirit.

Dr. F. Furman Kearley is one of the most studious men I know, and I know of no one with a more analytical and brilliant mind than Dr. Kearley. He loves the truth and the Lord's church.

When Dr. Kearley spoke on this subject, "God's Indwelling Spirit," there were so many favorable comments and requests for this lecture that I asked Dr. Kearley to put it in tract form that people might have the privilege of reading and meditating on this important subject.

Furman Kearley was born and reared in Montgomery, Ala. He finished high school and college at Alabama Christian College. He went on to higher institutions of learning and received his Ph. D. in Greek. Even though he holds possibly as many academic degrees as any man in the brotherhood, yet he is a very humble man and continues to preach the gospel in its purity and simplicity. His higher education has not made him haughty or arrogant but has caused him to have a deeper love and respect for God's word.

V. P. Black

ACKNOWLEDGMENTS

In writing this book, I have used much material that had previously been published in the form of books, pamphlets, and articles. I wish to express my appreciation to the publishing companies, editors, and authors listed in the Bibliography for their kind permission to quote portions of these works in their present form. Although the publishers, authors, and editors are too numerous to be listed here, I am deeply indebted to each and every one of them for their knowledge and assistance.

TABLE OF CONTENTS

Chapter

PREFACE

This study on the Holy Spirit and his indwelling is the result of twenty-five years of close study of God's word. I am deeply indebted to many great teachers who have shared their insights with me. Some whom I must mention are Rex Turner, Edd Holt, Leonard Johnson, R. C. White, W. B. West, Jr., E. H. Ijams, Jack Lewis, John Scott, James Bales, Franklin Camp and Gus Nichols. No doubt many others deserve much credit also. Therefore, I claim no originality but I do hope and pray that this study reflects the only infallible source, the word of God, and that the conclusions are in harmony with it.

The only justification for putting this into print is the fact that many have requested and urged that it be made available. I originally began this study for my benefit and understanding. Gradually I used it in sermons and classes. Soon, invitations came to speak on the subject at various places. Following these lectures, several would ask if copies were available. Finally, I was asked to speak on the Spring '74 lectureship of Alabama Christian College, my Alma Mater. Following the lecture, several people asked for copies. Brother V. P. Black suggested that I make it available for publication and let the proceeds go to Alabama Christian College. I am most happy to do this.

Every effort has been made to make this free of error. However, being human there will no doubt be some mistakes. I also felt the urge to revise it once more before sending it to press, but I remembered an admonition from Brother J. D. Bales, "If you wait until you feel perfect about a manuscript you will never get anything published." Therefore I have resisted the temptation. I pray that in spite of its shortcomings, this endeavor will provide some edification and enlightenment for its readers.

I would like to dedicate this effort to so many who have made me what I am: primarily, to my devoted and loving wife, Helen, who has helped me beyond description; secondly, to my Mother who headed me in the right direction; finally, to my teachers.

INTRODUCTION

Problem to be Solved

The problem of this study is what is the true and proper exposition of the doctrine of the indwelling of the Holy Spirit. Especially in regard to Romans 8:9, 11, what is meant by and how does the Spirit dwell in us? Since the Spirit does dwell in us what is meant by and how does he lead us, bear witness with us, help our infirmities and make intercession for the saints?

In seeking the solution to this problem and the answer to these questions, the procedure will require three main steps. The first is an examination of the history of the doctrine of the Holy Spirit to determine the main views and how they developed especially in the Restoration Movement. The second step involves presenting the general doctrine of the Holy Spirit. The third step is an analysis of Romans eight and other passages on the indwelling of the Holy Spirit and his operation in sanctification.

CHAPTER I
HISTORY OF THE DOCTRINE
OF THE HOLY SPIRIT

From Second Century through the Reformation

The nature, work, and operation of the Holy Spirit have long been subjects over which religious groups have been divided and Bible students have been confused. Since the early beginnings of Christianity there have been controversies over the trinity, its existence and nature. Most of the early writers admitted three persons in the trinity, God the Father, God the Son, and God the Holy Spirit [1] However, at least one group, the Monarchians, believed and taught that God, Christ, and the Holy Spirit were one person, and they admitted no personal distinction between them. [2]

Through the centuries the controversy has continued. Gregory of Nazianzus tells us that there was a great diversity of opinions among the theologians concerning the Spirit, who was variously regarded as an energy or influence, a creature or angelic being. Others thought it best not to make any definite statements concerning the Spirit. [3] The controversy for orthodox Christianity was fairly well resolved by the end of the second ecumenical council at Constantinople in 381. The resolving of this conflict and the role played by Athanasius is explained as follows:

> Athanasius, now in a later period of his life, again proved to be of service in the solution of this problem. He had become convinced that, if we are to hold to the Baptismal Formula, the Spirit cannot be a creature. If the Spirit is a creature, then something of a different nature is introduced into the Godhead, and we have a Diad instead of a Trinity. The Spirit, like the Son, must be *homoousios* (co-essential, con-substantial, same-natured). This he undertook to prove from His work of sanctification. Athanasius wrote on this subject in four letters *Ad*

---

1 All footnotes will be found at the end of the book on page 49-50.

Serapionem. Bishop Macedonia of Constantinople opposed this position and declared that the Holy Spirit is a creature subordinate to the Son. But a synod at Alexandria (362), presided over by Athanasius, established the *homoousia* of the Holy Spirit who was declared to be a person like the Father and the Son. The disciples of Macedonius were styled *Pneumatomachians* and later were called *Macedonians.* The leading theologians, such as the three Cappadocians and Didymus the Blind, followed in the footsteps of Athanasius. It was now the Baptismal Formula, taken directly from the Scriptures, which was the real moving factor in this direction. Cyril of Jerusalem had already taught the divinity of the Spirit as a person. The Cappadocians aided with detailed argumentation.

Thus it came to pass after the death of Athanasius (373) that the expressions on the Holy Spirit, as we have them in the present form of the Nicene Creed, were sanctioned at the so-called second ecumenical council at Constantinople (381). At a synod held in Rome (380) the Occident had already decided against all expressions of doubt with regard to the deity of the Spirit. The Spirit was now understood to be an *hypostassis*, like the Father and the Son. The Spirit's work was interpreted as the completion and application of Christ's redemptive work. The difference between the Son and the Spirit is this: The Son is generated and sent forth, while the Spirit proceeds. For a detailed study of the conception of the Holy Spirit in the age of the Fathers, see H. B. Swete, *The Holy Spirit in the Ancient Church,* 1912.[4]

However, though the question of the nature of the Holy Spirit was settled for most of Christianity, the question of the operation of the Spirit became very important in the Reformation and since. Lutheran theology in the Augsburg Confession stressed that "this righteousness, if experienced by the regenerated, is wrought in the heart when the Holy Ghost is received through the Word." [5] In contrast Zwingli and Calvin took the position that God can also, without previous preaching, extend grace to the soul through His Spirit. [6]Writing against the Lutherans on this subject Calvin said:

> But they do not consider that when the apostle makes hearing the source of faith, he only describes the ordinary economy and dispensation of the Lord, which He generally observes in the calling of the people; but he does not prescribe a perpetual rule, precluding His employment of any other method; which He has certainly employed in the calling of many to whom He has given the true knowledge of Himself in an internal manner, by the illumination of His Spirit, without the intervention of any preaching.[7]

The Anabaptists and others took even more extreme positions on the direct operation of the Holy Spirit, asserting that inner light was provided by the Spirit. During the seventeen and eighteen hundreds many spiritualistic and enthusiastic groups developed teaching that one must pray through, be baptized with the Spirit, etc. Such emotional gatherings as the Cane Ridge revival meetings were common. In these meetings people claimed to receive the Spirit and manifested it by screaming, shaking, or fainting.[8]

The Restoration Movement and
the Doctrine of the Holy Spirit

It was against this background that the Restoration Movement began. In an attempt to restore New Testament Christianity and to combat error many debates and discussions have been held and in many of them the propositions concerned the doctrine of the Holy Spirit. In general the denominations have held to the direct operation of the Holy Spirit apart from the word or with the word whereas debators for the church of Christ have held that the Spirit operates through the word.

To be more specific, in the *Hardeman-Bogard Debate,* [9] Mr. Ben M. Bogard affirmed the proposition, "The Bible teaches that in conviction and conversion the Holy Spirit exercises a power or influence in addition to the written or spoken word." Of course, Brother Hardeman denied and affirmed instead that the Spirit operates through the word. Again in the *Porter-Tingley Debate*, the *Nichols-Weaver Debate*, other debates as well as articles and tracts, the extreme views of the direct operation versus operation through the word have been expressed. Thus, the present position of many leaders in the Restoration Movement among churches of Christ may be summarized, in the opinion of this author, by the words of a very respected leader, H. Leo Boles:

> The Holy Spirit in no instance has dispensed with the truth, whether it be in the new birth or in the sanctification of saints. No man can intelligently and successfully affirm himself to be conscious of a divine fiat of the Holy Spirit that is not expressed by the word of God. The power of the Holy Spirit, both in conversion and sanctification, is so blended with the force of the word of God that no intelligent mind can separate them. No one can logically express an article of faith that does not come through the word of God. The Holy Spirit and the word of God are inseparable.[10]

Since this is the general conclusion of those in the Restoration Movement to this date, the task now is to reexamine this conclusion and the arguments for it in order to determine whether any modification is necessary for the complete restoration of New Testament doctrine. This will be done by first noticing the general doctrine of the Holy Spirit and then the doctrine of the indwelling of the Spirit in Romans eight and parallel passages.

CHAPTER II
THE DOCTRINE OF THE HOLY SPIRIT
The Holy Spirit is a Divine Being

Much of the misunderstanding, superstition, false doctrine and mysticism about the Holy Spirit comes about because he is not thought of as a divine being like God who is Spirit and Christ who is Spirit also. The fact that the King James Version uses the term "Holy Ghost" eighty-nine times [11] in reference to him has led some to think of him mysteriously as a ghost of which people are frightened. The Holy Spirit is not an "it" but a masculine person as seen by the following facts.

Masculine Singular Terms

ekeinos —This demonstrative pronoun which is literally translated "that male person" is masculine singular nominative. [12] It is used in John 14:26; 15:26; 16:8, 13, 14 and elsewhere. Vine says its use marks special distinction [13] and this form of emphasis should always be noted.

auton —This is the accusative singular masculine form of the personal pronoun meaning he, she, it. In this form, being an object in the sentence of John 16:7, it must mean "him."

pneuma —Though this word for spirit is itself neuter and takes neuter pronouns, yet the word does not signify the gender of that to which it is applied. Many Greek words such as the words for world, road, desert are masculine or feminine but really these are neuter in gender. Marshall commenting on this says, "The gender of these pronouns agrees, of course, with the antecedent *pneuma* (neuter); and this has been kept though the personal Spirit of God is meant. Elsewhere, masculine pronouns are in fact used."[14]

Therefore, the Holy Spirit is a masculine person the same as God and Christ. The translators are agreed in ascribing to him as masculine personality.

The Holy Spirit Has Personal Actions

He speaks. "But the Spirit saith expressly that in later times some shall fall away from the faith." (I Tim. 4:1.)

He testifies. "But when the Comforter is come, whom I will send unto you from the Father, even the Spirit of truth, which proceedeth from the Father, he shall bear witness of me." (John 15:26.)

He teaches and quickens. "But the Comforter, even the Holy Spirit, whom the Father will send in my name, he shall teach you all things, and bring to your remembrance all that I said unto you." (John 14:26.)

He guides. "Howbeit when he, the Spirit of truth, is come, he shall guide you into all the truth." (John 16:13.)

He leads and forbids. "And they went through the region of Phrygia and Galatia, having been forbidden of the Holy Spirit to speak the work in Asia; and when they were come over against Mysia, they assayed to go into Bithynia; and the Spirit of Jesus suffered them not." (Acts 16:6, 7.)

He searches. "But unto us God revealed them through the Spirit: for the Spirit searcheth all things, yea, the deep things of God." (I Cor. 2:10.) [15]

The Holy Spirit Has Definite Personal Traits

Mind: "And he that searcheth the hearts knoweth what is the mind of the Spirit, because he maketh intercession for the saints according to the will of God." (Rom. 8:27.)

Knowledge: "For who among men knoweth the things of a man, save the spirit of the man, which is in him? Even so the things of God none knoweth; save the Spirit of God." (I Cor. 2:11.)

Affections: "Now I beseech you, brethren, by our Lord Jesus Christ, and by the love of the Spirit, that ye strive together with me in your prayers to God for me." (Rom. 15:30.)

Will: "But all these worketh the one and the same Spirit, dividing to each one severally even as he will." (I Cor. 12:11.)

Goodness: "Thou gavest also thy good Spirit to instruct them, and withheldest not thy manna from their mouth." (Neh. 9:20.) [16]

The Holy Spirit Suffers Slights and Injuries

He can be grieved and vexed. "And grieve not the Holy Spirit of God, in whom ye were sealed unto the day of redemption." (Eph. 4:30.)

He can be despised. "Of how much sorer punishment, think ye, shall he be judged worthy, who hath trodden under foot the Son of God, and hath counted the blood of the covenant wherewith he was sanctified an unholy thing, and hath done despite unto the Spirit of grace?" (Heb. 10:29.)

He can be blasphemed. "Every sin and blasphemy shall be forgiven unto men: but the blasphemy against the Spirit shall not be forgiven." (Matt. 12:31.)

He can be resisted. "Ye stiffnecked and uncircumcised in heart and ears, ye do always resist the Holy Spirit: as your fathers did, so do ye." (Acts 7:51.)

He can be lied to. "Why hath Satan filled thy heart to lie to the Holy Spirit, and to keep back part of the price of the land?" (Acts 5:3.) [17]

The Holy Spirit Has Divine Personality Traits

He is eternal. "How much more shall the blood of Christ, who through the eternal Spirit offered himself without blemish unto God, cleanse your conscience from dead works to serve the living God?" (Heb. 9:14.)

He is omniscient. "But unto us God revealed them through the Spirit: for the Spirit searcheth all things, yea, the deep things of God. For who among men knoweth the things of a man, save the spirit of the man, which is in him? Even so the things of God none knoweth, save the Spirit of God." (I Cor. 2:10, 11.)

He is omnipotent. "But as for me, I am full of power by the Spirit of Jehovah, and of judgment, and of might to declare unto Jacob his transgression, and to Israel his sin." (Micah 3:8.)

He is omnipresent. "Whither shall I go from thy Spirit? Or whither shall I flee from thy presence?" (Ps. 139:7.) [18]

The Holy Spirit Does Divine Works

He had a part in creation. When the earth was waste and void, and darkness was upon the face of the deep, "the Spirit of God moved upon the face of the waters. And God said, Let there be light: and there was light." (Gen. 1:2, 3.) "By his Spirit the heavens are garnished." (Job 26:13.)

His providence also is evidenced in tender care over the works of creation. "Thou sendest forth thy Spirit, they are created; and thou renewest the face of the ground." (Ps. 104:30.)

He has a part in regeneration, for we read in John 3:5: "Except one be born of water and the Spirit, he cannot enter into the kingdom of God."

The Holy Spirit is involved in the resurrection. "But if the Spirit of him that raised up Jesus from the dead dwelleth in you, he that raised up Christ Jesus from the dead shall give life also to your mortal bodies through his Spirit that dwelleth in you." (Rom. 8:11.)[19]

The Holy Spirit Is One of the Trinity

This fact is proved by a multitude of passages. In many of these passages the three are manifested as different beings by both location and action. Notice the following passages:

Matt. 3:16, 17—And Jesus, when he was baptized, went up straightway from the water: and lo, the heavens were opened unto him, and he saw the Spirit of God descending as a dove, and coming upon him; and lo, a voice out of the heavens, saying, This is my beloved Son, in whom I am well pleased.

John 14:16, 17—And I will pray the Father, and he shall give you another Comforter, that he may be with you for ever, even the Spirit of truth: whom the world cannot receive; for it beholdeth him not, neither knoweth him: ye know him; for he abideth with you, and shall be in you.

The Holy Spirit Has Special Division of Labor

Though there may not be a complete distinction in the work or labor of the Godhead, there is a definite trend. In creation and redemption, God is the planner. (Eph. 3:8-12.) Christ executed the creation and the redemption of man. (John 1:1-3; Eph. 1:3-14.) The Holy Spirit beautified or finished the creation, (Job 26:13; 33:4.) and he revealed the plan of salvation to all men. (Eph. 3:1-7.) Jesus indicated that the Holy Spirit would come in his place to comfort and aid the disciples. (John 14:16-18.) The Holy Spirit then finished the work which was begun by Jesus. Thus, the Godhead has always been and is united in working toward the same goal, yet, in certain respects, they work independently in order to carry out the plan. [20]

The Holy Spirit as Distinguished from His Works

It is necessary to recognize the Holy Spirit as a divine being in order to distinguish between him and his power, between the Giver and his gifts. The Spirit himself, as a divine person, is the one who imparts or gives certain powers and gifts. The various gifts are not the Holy Spirit himself but are manifestations of the Spirit. This is the idea presented in I Corinthians 12:4-11. One writer maintains that the Greek New Testament shows a clear distinction between the Giver and his gifts. He states that *pneuma hagion* without the definite article refers to the holy gift or power but when the definite article is used it refers to the Holy Giver. Thus Acts 2:4 would be rendered, "And they were all filled with (of) holy gift (spirit), and began to speak with other tongues as the Giver (Spirit) gave them utterance." 21 Whether this distinction will hold up completely or only in part this writer is not prepared to say. However, it does illustrate the point that the Holy Spirit is a divine person who gives certain powers or gifts to Christians.

Thus, we have learned that the Holy Spirit is a divine person who gives divine gifts. Next, we must consider the question, does the Holy Giver give gifts in different amounts or measures? Are spiritual gifts to be equated with baptism of the Spirit, filled with the Spirit, etc.?

Measures of the Spirit's Gifts

The only time the word measure is used in direct reference to the Spirit is in John 3:34. It is translated in the A. V. in these words, "For he whom God hath sent speaketh the words of God: for God giveth not the Spirit by measure (*unto him*)." The A. R. V. translated it just the same except that it omits the italicized phrase, unto him. This passage is discussed much in studying whether there are different measures of the Spirit's gifts.

Some religious groups maintain that all the Spirit's gifts were of the same degree. They contend that the baptism of the Spirit, the gift of the Spirit (Acts 2:38), the like gift (Acts 11:17), being full of the Spirit and the spiritual gifts (I Cor. 12:1-11) all refer to the same thing and were equal in power. These contend that John 3:34 means that God gives not the Spirit by measure to anyone, but that all receive the same measure of the Spirit.

Others maintain that there is a difference between baptism of the Spirit, the gift of the Spirit (Acts 2:38) and spiritual gifts. These contend that John 3:34 means that God gives not the Spirit by measure unto Christ. There are also various other opinions, but they would in most respects be similar to one of these two.

Now, how shall we solve this problem and understand if there is a difference in the measure of the Spirit's gifts? First of all, the Greek scholars can help us but little because "unto him" of "Christ" is not in the Greek text and for the most part it would simply be arraying scholarship against scholarship on the grammatical problems of the text. The same problem that exists in the English translations exists in the Greek text. Secondly, reading the context from verse 31 through 36 does not definitely determine whether verse 34 refers to Christ alone receiving the Spirit without measure, or to others generally. However, the context is talking mainly about the Father and the Son.

The third possible solution is to study the different expressions referring to the Spirit's gifts to see if there is any difference in them and to see if any received the Spirit by measure.

Christ Had Spirit Without Measure

Whatever else John 3:34 refers to, all agree that Christ had the Spirit's gifts without measure. Verse 35 says, "The Father loveth the Son, and hath given all things into his hand." Christ's power was not limited in the performance of miracles. He could heal from the simplest ailments to even raising the dead. He had all power and could call twelve legions of angels to protect him. (Matt. 26:53.)

The Baptism in the Spirit

The term baptism in or with the Holy Spirit occurs in the New Testament six times, [22] and each time it is uttered in the form of a promise, never a command. Also, in Joel 2:28-32 it is a promise. It is further referred to as a gift. (Acts 11:16, 17.) Now to whom was this gift of the baptism in the Spirit promised? Joel said "all flesh" and

John said "you." However, Christ said the world could not receive the Spirit. (John 14:17.) "All flesh" unless limited would include sinners. The "you" to whom John the Baptist was speaking included those whom he called "Ye offspring of vipers." (Matt. 3:7.) Therefore, these terms must be limited. When Christ spoke of the baptism in the Spirit he promised it to the apostles (Acts 1:5) and to the Gentiles at the household of Cornelius. (Acts 11:16, 17.) These two groups, being made up of Jews and Gentiles, fulfilled the promise to "all flesh" since they represented all flesh. The Bible tells of no others being baptized in the Spirit. [23]

Further, the baptism in the Spirit was to be administered by Christ according to the promises. Peter states that Christ fulfilled the promises in Acts 2:33, "And having received of the Father the promise of the Holy Spirit, he hath poured forth this, which ye see and hear."

Next, the power given by baptism in the Spirit must be determined. The following outline will show what the Holy Spirit enabled the apostles to do.

1. He enabled the apostles to teach the whole will of the Lord and prophesy. (John 14:26; 15:26; 16:13; Acts 1:8; 2:1-4.)

2. He enabled them to confirm the word with miracles, even to raising the dead. (Mark 16:20; Acts 9:36-43.)

3. He enabled them to speak, without study, lessons and foreign languages. (Luke 21:14, 15; Acts 2:1-4.)

4. He enabled them to impart spiritual gifts to others. (Acts 8:14-17; 19:1-7; Rom. 1:11.) [24]

However, it is immediately noticed that the Holy Spirit did not give them power equal to Christ who has all authority in heaven and on earth (Matt. 28:18-20), who is head over all things to the church including the apostles. (Eph. 1:21-23; 4:11-13.) The baptism in the Spirit did not enable the apostles to administer Spirit baptism to others.

Therefore, the apostles did not have an equal amount or measure of the Spirit with Christ.

Spiritual Gifts

The term spiritual gifts is used in the New Testament four times and these gifts are referred to many other times.[25]

First, we note that this term was never used in the promises concerning the Holy Spirit and his gifts. Spiritual gifts must have been included in the general promises concerning the Holy Spirit. (Luke 11:13; John 7:39.)

Spiritual gifts were administered by the apostles. Paul said in Romans 1:11, "For I long to see you, that I may impart unto you some spiritual gift, to the end ye may be established." This passage offers strong proof that only the apostles could impart spiritual gifts. There were already in Rome those who possessed these gifts (Rom. 12:3-8), but they could not impart them to others, else there would have been no need for Paul to do so. There were, also, some strong and notable Christians at Rome who had been associated with the apostles in other places, such as Aquila and Priscilla (Rom. 16:3-15), yet, they could not impart spiritual gifts. Paul also imparted spiritual gifts to the twelve men at Ephesus (Acts 19:1-7) and Timothy (II Tim. 1:6) through the laying on of his hands.

However, some argue that the case of Timothy proves that others besides the apostles could impart spiritual gifts. They refer to I Timothy 4:14 where Paul says, "Neglect not the gift that is in thee, which was given thee by prophecy, with the laying on of the hands of the presbytery." These contend that Timothy received one gift from Paul and another from the presbytery. This is highly improbable, for Paul guided by inspired wisdom and possessing the power to impart all the gifts, would have certainly given Timothy all the gifts he needed. The true explanation is found in two Greek prepositions, *dia* (II Tim. 1:6) meaning through or by the means of [26] and *meta* (I Tim. 4:14) meaning with, together with or accompanied by. [27] Thus, it is easily seen that Paul as an apostle was the instrument through whom the gift was bestowed and that the presbytery, at the same occasion, laid their hands on Timothy together with Paul, not to impart gifts but as a gesture of commendation. (Acts 13:1-3.)

Those who possessed spiritual gifts were not able to do all that the apostles could do. Some could prophesy, others could heal, others could speak in tongues, etc. As a rule one person would have only one gift. (I Cor. 12:1-11.) However, it seems that evangelists had several gifts combined. (Acts 6:5-10; 8:5-13; 21:8.) No one, though, with spiritual gifts could impart spiritual gifts to others. (Acts 8:14-24.)

Thus, spiritual gifts were different from Holy Spirit baptism in that the apostles administered it instead of Christ, those with spiritual gifts could not do all the works the apostles could and they could not impart spiritual gifts to others as the apostles could. 28

Indwelling Gift of the Holy Spirit

Already, three measures of the Spirit's gifts have been studied, and all of them gave miraculous power. Now, it must be determined whether "gift of the Holy Spirit" (Acts 2:38) is the same as spiritual gifts discussed in I Corinthians 12:1-11. Some contend that wherever the word gift is used in reference to the spirit, it is the same gift; others say it is not.

The gift of the Holy Spirit (Acts 2:38) was promised to all who believed, repented and were baptized. (Acts 2:36-38.) Further, the Holy Spirit was given to all who obeyed God (Acts 5:32.) Thus, this gift of the Spirit was given to all who obeyed the gospel, automatically, whereas spiritual gifts had to be imparted. (Rom. 1:11.) Also, this gift of the Holy Spirit did not give any miraculous power such as the apostles and those with spiritual gifts had. This fact is self-evident from the fact that all Christians did not do miraculous deeds and from Paul's statement in I Corinthians 12:29. Thus, the gift of the Holy Spirit (Acts 2:38) seems to be equated with the indwelling of the Spirit. (Rom. 8:9-11; I Cor. 3:16; 6:19; Gal. 4:6; Jam. 4:5.)

Filled with the Spirit

Many are confused by the expression "filled with the Spirit," thinking that since it is used to refer to all the previously mentioned gifts it makes them all to be the same measure. Christ was "full of the Holy Spirit." (Luke 4:1.) The same is said of the apostles (Acts 2:4), Peter (Acts 4:8) and Paul (Acts 13:9) in particular, who were baptized in the Spirit. It is also used in reference to those with spiritual gifts as Stephen and Barnabas. (Acts 13:52; Eph. 5:18.) The expression is used at least fifteen times in the New Testament. [29]

Probably the most troublesome passage is Acts 9:17 where Ananias said to Saul, "The Lord . . .hath sent me, that thou mayest receive thy sight, and be filled with the Holy Spirit." Some take this to mean the baptism in the Spirit and make Ananias the administrator. This cannot be proven. There are three Greek words translated filled in these passages, *pletho*—eight times and *pleres* and its verb from *pleroo*—seven times. These words have as their meaning to be under the influence of, to fully influence. [30] This is the sense in which filled is used. This is well illustrated by Acts 13:52, "And the disciples were filled with joy and with the Holy Spirit." They were under the influence of joy and in the same way, of the Holy Spirit. Thus, when people were filled with the Spirit, they were guided or influenced by the Spirit, yet that could be in different degrees. Most probably, Ananias was speaking of being filled with the gift of the Holy Spirit that Peter spake of (Acts 2:38) since he uttered the command to be baptized (Acts 22:16) just as Peter did on Pentecost.

Summary

Therefore, the scriptures definitely teach that there are different degrees or measures of the Spirit's gifts. Only Christ had the Spirit without measure; others have it by measure. Also, God's word shows a distinction between the Spirit and his gifts. With this general view of the Holy Spirit and his gifts in mind, the foundation for the exposition of the indwelling of the Holy Spirit and his work in sanctification as discussed in Romans eight has now been laid.

CHAPTER III
HOW THE HOLY SPIRIT DWELLS
IN THE CHRISTIAN

Theories Concerning the Indwelling

The question, "How does the Holy Spirit dwell in the Christian?" has been a source of discussion and controversy throughout the history of the church. Many different views or theories have been advocated. Some of the major ones are as follows:

1. The Holy Spirit does not dwell in humans at all.

2. The Holy Spirit dwells representatively by the word.

3. The Holy Spirit dwells in a miraculous measure and empowers to speak in tongues, perform miracles, etc. (Position of Neo-Pentecostals).

4. The Holy Spirit dwells in the Christian effecting salvation and sanctification through irresistable grace and impossibility of apostasy.

5. The Holy Spirit dwells in the Christian literally or actually in a personal manner, that is in his own person, but this indwelling is completely non-miraculous and in no way makes further revelation of truth or interferes with free, moral agency.

Some would argue that it makes no difference how the Holy Spirit dwells in the Christian, just so long as we all agree the Holy Spirit does dwell in us. This may be true with respect to some views. However, some of the theories mentioned above clearly deny other plain scriptures and thus contradict the word of God. Therefore, it is important that we give some consideration to how the Holy Spirit dwells in the Christian and especially we must be sure that any theory we may hold as to how the Spirit dwells in us does not contradict God's word and lead us into doctrines and practices that are erroneous. Therefore, it is the purpose of this paper (1) to examine what the scriptures say about the indwelling of the Holy Spirit, (2) to refute erroneous theories, and (3) to present a concept of how the Spirit dwells in the Christian that is in complete harmony with God's word.

Affirmations Concerning the Indwelling of the Spirit

The scriptures clearly and repeatedly affirm that the Holy Spirit dwells in the Christian. An examination of the scriptures affirming the indwelling of the Spirit is in order. The best way to study them is by arranging them according to the different Greek words used to express the dwelling or indwelling. The Greek word *oikeo* (οἰκέω) is used three times:

1. **Romans 8:9-11**—"But ye are not in the flesh but in the Spirit, if so be that the Spirit of God dwelleth (oikei) in you. But if any man hath not the Spirit of Christ, he is none of his. And if Christ is in you, the body is dead because of sin; but the spirit is life because of righteousness. But if the Spirit of him that raised up Jesus from the dead dwelleth (oikei) in you, he that raised up Christ Jesus from the dead shall give life also to your mortal bodies through his Spirit that dwelleth in you." (ASV)

2. **I Corinthians 3:16**—"Know ye not that ye are a temple of God, and that the Spirit of God dwelleth in you?" (ASV)

The Greek word *enoikeo* (ἐνοικέω) is used twice.

1. **Romans 8:11**—"But if the Spirit of him that raised up Jesus from the dead dwelleth in you, he that raised up Christ Jesus from the dead shall give life also to your mortal bodies through his Spirit that dwelleth (enoikeo) in you." (ASV)

2. **II Timothy 1:14**—"That good thing which was committed unto thee guard through the Holy Spirit which dwelleth (enoikeo) in us." (ASV)

Two other passages are often used in this discussion. John 14:16, 17, 23, which speaks of the Holy Spirit dwelling in the apostles is the first. The other is James 4:5 which some believe is speaking of the dwelling of the human spirit. These passages will not be used in this discussion.

The above passages affirm that the Holy Spirit dwells in Christians, both collectively and individually. The plural forms of the Greek pronoun for "you" and "us" are used in several of the passages. However, Romans 8:9 clearly uses singular pronouns to make it plain that the Holy Spirit dwells in each individual as well as in the church community collectively. Therefore, it is impossible to believe the scriptures and at the same time to deny that the Holy Spirit dwells in Christians in some manner. This is further confirmed by a study of the "gift of the Holy Spirit."

The Gift of the Holy Spirit

The scriptures teach that the gift of the Holy Spirit in Acts 2:38 is the gift or indwelling of the Holy Spirit in the Christian as the following examination of the phrase "the gift of the Holy Spirit" demonstrates.

The term, "the gift of the Holy Spirit" is used twice in the New Testament. The passages read as follows:

Acts 2:38—"And Peter said unto them, Repent ye, and be baptized every one of you in the name of Jesus Christ unto the remission of your sins; and ye shall receive the gift of the Holy Spirit." (ASV)

Acts 10:44-47—"While Peter yet spake these words, the Holy Spirit fell on all them that heard the word. (45) And they of the circumcision that believed were amazed, as many as came with Peter, because that on the Gentiles also was poured out the gift of the Holy Spirit. (46) For they heard them speak with tongues, and magnify God. Then answered Peter, (47) Can any man forbid the water, that these should not be baptized, who have received the Holy Spirit as well as we?" (ASV)

In Acts 2:38 it is not clear whether the phrase "of the Holy Spirit" is a subjective genitive or an objective genitive. That is, whether it is a gift which the Holy Spirit gives, or if the Holy Spirit himself is the gift. However, in Acts 10:44-47 it is clear that the Holy Spirit is the gift.

1. Acts 10:44 observes that the Holy Spirit fell on the ones hearing.

2. Acts 10:45 affirms that the gift of the Holy Spirit had been poured out on the Gentiles.

3. Acts 10:46 indicates that the Gentiles were empowered to speak in tongues by the gift of the Holy Spirit.

4. Acts 10:47 relates that Peter said the Gentiles had received the Holy Spirit as the apostles did.

Therefore in Acts 10:45 the gift of the Holy Spirit is an objective genitive and the Holy Spirit himself is the gift. The question of whether "the gift of the Holy Spirit" in these passages is the same or a different manifestation of the Holy Spirit is another question. However, the grammar of the two is the same and the Holy Spirit is the gift himself.

Parallel passages further indicate that "the gift of the Holy Spirit" is an objective genitive and that the Holy Spirit is the gift. Consider the following:

1. **Acts 2:33**—"Being therefore, by the right hand of God exalted, and having received of the Father the promise of the

Holy Spirit, he hath poured forth this, which ye see and hear." (ASV)

This verse indicates that Jesus received the promise of the Holy Spirit. That is, God poured out the Holy Spirit himself on the day of Pentecost, thus fulfilling the promise made by Jesus not to leave the apostles comfortless, but to send the Holy Spirit. (See John 14:16-18, Acts 1:8 and 2:1-4.)

2. **Galatians 3:14**—"That upon the Gentiles might come the blessing of Abraham in Christ Jesus; that we might receive the promise of the Spirit through faith." (ASV)

"The promise of the Spirit through faith" is the promise made by Joel that the Spirit would be poured out upon all flesh. (Joel 2:28-32.)

3. **II Corinthians 1:22**—"Who also sealed us, and gave us the earnest of the Spirit in our hearts." (ASV)

The phrase "gave us the earnest of the Spirit" is certainly an objective genitive affirming that the Spirit himself is the earnest given.

4. **II Corinthians 5:5**—"Now he that wrought us for this very thing is God, who gave unto us the earnest of the Spirit." (ASV)

This is exactly the same as the above passage.

5. **Ephesians 1:13**—"In whom ye also, having heard the word of the truth, the gospel of your salvation,—in whom, having also believed, ye were sealed with the Holy Spirit of promise." (ASV)

The term "the Holy Spirit of promise" makes clear that the Holy Spirit himself was promised by God and Christ to be with the Christians in the present economy of the Christian age.

6. **Ephesians 1:14**—"Which is an earnest of our inheritance, unto the redemption of God's own possession, unto the praise of his glory." (ASV)

This verse makes perfectly clear that the Holy Spirit is the earnest or down payment given and further shows that II Corinthians 1:22 and 5:5 are objective genitives.

7. **Hebrews 9:15**—"And for this cause he is the mediator of a new covenant, that a death having taken place for the redemption of the transgressions that were under the first covenant, they that have been called may receive the promise of the eternal inheritance." (ASV)

The phrase, "the promise of the eternal inheritance" is a parallel genitive construction, and it is clearly an objective genitive, that is, the promise is eternal inheritance.

8. **Revelation 14:11**—"And the smoke of their torment goeth up for ever and ever; and they have no rest day and night, they that worship the beast and his image and whoso receiveth the mark of his name." (ASV)

His name was the mark to be received.

9. **Romans 4:11**—"And he received the sign of circumcision, a seal of the righteousness of the faith which he had while he was in uncircumcision: that he might be the father of all them that believe, though they be in uncircumcision, that righteousness might be reckoned unto them." (ASV)

Here, circumcision was the sign and not the source or origin out of which the sign came.

10. **James 1:12**—"Blessed is the man that endureth temptation; for when he hath been approved, he shall receive the crown of life, which the Lord promised to them that love Him." (ASV)

11. **II Timothy 4:8**—"Henceforth there is laid up for me the crown of righteousness, which the Lord, the righteous judge, shall give to me at that day; and not to me only, but also to all them that have loved his appearing." (ASV)

Other passages clearly affirm that the Holy Spirit is the gift given by God to all his children, or Christians generally.

1. **Luke 11:13**—"If ye then, being evil, know how to give good gifts unto your children, how much more shall your heavenly Father give the Holy Spirit to them that ask him?" (ASV)

2. **Acts 5:32**—"And we are witnesses of these things; and so is the Holy Spirit whom God hath given to them that obey him." (ASV)

3. **I Corinthians 6:19**—"Or know ye not that your body is a temple of the Holy Spirit which is in you, which ye have from God? and ye are not your own." (ASV)

4. **II Corinthians 1:22**—"Who also sealed us, and gave us the earnest of the Spirit in our hearts." (ASV)

5. **Galatians 4:6**—"And because ye are sons, God sent forth the Spirit of his Son into our hearts, crying, Abba Father." (ASV)

6. **I Thessalonians 4:8**—"Therefore he that rejecteth, rejecteth not man, but God, who giveth His Holy Spirit unto you." (ASV)

Observations on the passages quoted above show clearly that the Holy Spirit was given to all Christians who obeyed the Lord. The Spirit was to dwell in and be with them.

1. The above passages clearly teach that the Holy Spirit was universally given to all who became Christians, children of

God, as a result of obeying His gospel and as a seal, or earnest, of their salvation.

2.   These passages are exactly parallel to the promise of Acts 2:38, and show that the Holy Spirit himself was given to all who believed, repented, and were baptized.

3.   In all of these instances, the gift of the Holy Spirit did not confer the power for miracles, for no one affirms that every Christian could perform miracles. Yet every Christian (obedient child of God) at Jerusalem, at Corinth, in Galatia, and in Thessalonica had the gift of the Holy Spirit.

4.   Therefore, the gift of the Holy Spirit in Acts 2:38 is a non-miraculous manifestation of the Holy Spirit given in fulfillment of the promise to all who repent and are baptized.

5.   Surely, no one affirms that all who repent and are baptized receive a miraculous manifestation of the Holy Spirit.

6.   Yet all who obey Acts 2:38 do receive the non-miraculous or indwelling manifestation of the Holy Spirit.

7.   Romans 8:9-11 affirms that if one does not have this Spirit, he is not Christ's. Therefore, every true Christian has the Spirit dwelling in him.

Definition of the Words Translated "Dwell"

A study of the Greek words used to describe the dwelling of the Holy Spirit clearly indicates that the Spirit dwelling in the Christian is real or actual. There are three forms of the same basic Greek word. The following examination of the words in their various contexts clearly sets forth the meaning of the words.

Parallel passages using the Greek word *oikeo* (οἰκέω) are:

1. **I Corinthians 3:16**—"Know ye not that ye are a temple of God, and that the Spirit of God dwelleth in you?" (ASV)

How does the Spirit dwell in the church collectively?

2. **Romans 7:17, 20**—"So now it is no more I that do it, but sin which dwelleth in me." (20) "But if what I would not, that I do, it is no more I that do it, but sin which dwelleth in me." (ASV)

How does sin dwell in us?

Parallel passages using the Greek word *enoikeo* (ἐνοικέω) are:

1. **Colossians 3:16**—"Let the word of Christ dwell in you richly; in all wisdom teaching and admonishing one another with psalms and hymns and spiritual songs, singing with grace in your hearts unto God." (ASV)

How does Christ's word dwell in you?

2. **II Corinthians 6:16**—"And what agreement hath a temple of God with idols? for we are a temple of the living God: even as God said, I will dwell in them, and walk in them: and I will be their God, and they shall be my people." (ASV)

How does God dwell in us?

Parallel passages using the Greek word *katoikeo* (κατοικέω) are listed below. Though this word is not used directly of the Holy Spirit's dwelling, it is definitely a parallel word.

1. **Matthew 4:13**—"And leaving Nazareth, he came and dwelt in Capernaum, which is by the sea, in the borders of Zebulun and Naphtali:" (ASV)

How did Jesus dwell in Capernaum?

2.   Matthew 12:43-45—"But the unclean spirit, when he is gone out of the man, passeth through waterless places, seeking rest, and findeth it not. (44) Then he saith, I will return into my house whence I came out; and when he is come, he findeth it empty, swept and garnished. (45) Then goeth he, and taketh with himself seven other spirits more evil than himself, and they enter in and dwell there: and the last state of that man becometh worse than the first. Even so shall it be also unto this evil generation." (ASV)

How did the unclean spirits dwell in the man? (See also Luke 11:24-26.)

3.   II Peter 3:13—"But, according to his promise, we look for new heavens and a new earth, wherein dwelleth righteousness." (ASV)

How will righteousness dwell in the new heaven and the new earth?

4.   James 4:5—"Or think ye that the scripture speaketh in vain? Doth the spirit which he made to dwell in us long unto envying?" (ASV)

How does the human spirit dwell within our bodies?

5.   Ephesians 3:17—"That Christ may dwell in your hearts through faith; to the end that ye, being rooted and grounded in love." (ASV)

How does Christ dwell in Christians?

The basic principles governing the use and interpretation of words must be followed if truth is to be understood. Some important principles have been stated concerning the interpretation and definition of words. The three following quotes are significant.

1. M. S. Terry in *Biblical Hermeneutics*, p. 159 has observed "Words should be taken in their literal sense unless such literal interpretation involves a manifest contradiction or absurdity."

2. Moses E. Lard, in *Lard's Quarterly*, Vol. I, March 1864, p. 236, wrote: "A word, whenever met with, is to be taken in its common current sense, unless the subject-matter, the context, or a qualifying epithet forbids it."

3. Brother Gus Nichols, in his *Lectures on the Holy Spirit,* pp. 166, 167 observed: "If God had wanted to tell us that the Holy Spirit is really and actually in us, as Christians, how could he have chosen words more effective for the purpose than he has used?"

The Greek Lexicographers give us a clear concept of the meanings and uses of the Greek words under consideration.

1. Of *oikeo* Vine says: to dwell (from oikos, a house), to inhabit as one's abode, is derived from the Sanskrit, vic, a dwelling place (the Eng. termination—wick is connected). It is used (a) of God as dwelling in light, I Tim. 6:16; (b) of the indwelling of the Spirit of God in the believer, Rom. 8:9, 11, or in a church, I Cor. 3:16; (c) of the indwelling of sin, Rom. 7:20; (d) of the absence of any good thing in the flesh of the believer, Rom. 7:18; (e) of the dwelling together of those who are married, I Corinthians 7:12, 13." [31]

2. Of *katoikeo* Vines observes: "kata, down, and No. 1, the most frequent verb with this meaning, properly signifies to settle down in a dwelling, to dwell fixedly in a place. Besides its literal sense, it is used of (a) the indwelling of the totality of the attributes and powers of the Godhead in Christ, Col.

1:19; 2:9; (b) the indwelling of Christ in the hearts of believers ('may make a home in your hearts'), Eph. 3:17; (c) the dwelling of Satan in a locality, Rev. 2:13; (d) the future indwelling of righteousness in the new heavens and earth, 2 Pet. 3:13. It is translated "dwellers" in Acts 1:19; 2:9; "inhabitants" in Rev. 17:2, A. V. (R. V., "they that dwell"), "inhabiters" in Rev. 8:13 and 12:12, A. V. (R. V., "them that dwell"). " [32]

3. Regarding *enoikeo*, Vine observes: "lit., to dwell in (en, in, and No. 1) is used, with a spiritual significance only, of (a) the indwelling of God in believers, II Cor. 6:16; (b) the indwelling of the Holy Spirit, Rom. 8:11, 2 Tim. 1:14; (c) the indwelling of the word of Christ, Col. 3:16; (d) the indwelling of faith, 2 Tim. 1:5; (e) the indwelling of sin in the believer, Rom. 7:17." [33]

4. Gerhard Kittle's *Theological Workbook of the New Testament*, says the following concerning *oikeo:* "More important, however, is the fact that *oikein* is used to describe inward psychological and spiritual processes. Thus Dg. 6, 3a can say metaphorically: . . .(as the soul lives in the body, but does not derive from the body, so is the relation of Christians in the world). Similarly we read in R. 7:18: "For I know that in me (that is, in my flesh) dwelleth no good thing: . . .and 7:20 goes on to say that sin dwells in me . . .The dwelling of sin in man denotes its dominion over him, its lasting connection with his flesh, and yet also a certain distinction from it. The sin which dwells in me . . .is no passing guest, but by its continuous presence becomes the master of the house. (cf. Str.–B., III, 239). Paul can speak in just the same way, however, of the lordship of the Spirit. The community knows . . .that the Spirit of God dwells in the new man . . .(I C. 3:16; R. 8:9, 11). This "dwelling" is more than ecstatic rapture or impulsion by a superior power. The spiritual part of man is not set aside, but impressed into service. The use of the same formula . . .in I C. 3:16 and R. 8:9, 11 suggests that

it was one of the permanent catechetical and didactic elements in Paul's theology. [34]

An examination of how the King James translators translated the Greek word shows further the clear, general sense of the word.

1.   *OIKEO* is translated by the A. V. "dwell" nine times.

2.   *ENOIKEO* is translated by the A. V. "dwell in" five times.

3.   *KATOIKEO* is translated by the A. V. "dwell" 35; "dwell at", 4; "dwell in", 4; "dweller at", 1; "dweller in", 1; "inhabitant", 1; "inhabiter", 1; "inhabiter of", 1.

Thus, from an examination of the Greek words to describe the indwelling of the Holy Spirit, there is no reason not to take them in their general sense. Thus, the Bible affirms that the Holy Spirit dwells in the Christian. The Bible also teaches that God, Christ, Satan, unclean spirits, sin, or the human spirit dwell in people. Nowhere does the Bible explain exactly how. But we must accept the fact of the indwelling just as surely as we accept the fact of the indwelling of sin or unclean spirits.

An Examination of Various Theories Concerning the Indwelling of the Holy Spirit

The scriptures clearly indicate that the gift of the Holy Spirit, or the indwelling measure of the Holy Spirit which first century Christians had, did not empower them to perform miracles and make revelations. The gift, or indwelling manifestation of the Holy Spirit was non-miraculous. Therefore, the Pentecostal and Neo-Pentecostal theories concerning the gift or indwelling of the Holy Spirit, being of a miraculous nature, have no support from the scriptures. This is proven by the following observations.

1.   According to Romans 1:11, the Christians at Rome were lacking in some miraculous spiritual gifts. Yet these

Christians had fulfilled Acts 2:38 and therefore had already received the promise of Acts 2:38, that is the earnest and sealing of the Holy Spirit.

2. The Christians at Samaria needed Peter and John to come down to impart miraculous spiritual gifts. However, since they had already repented and been baptized, they already had received the gift of the Holy Spirit which must have been non-miraculous. (Acts 8:1-24.)

3. Since miraculous manifestations of the Holy Spirit were only obtained through the laying on of the apostles hands or through the direct baptism in the Spirit by Jesus and since the apostles could not possibly, physically go personally to every Christian converted in the first century, therefore the Christians in general did not have a miraculous manifestation of the Spirit, but the non-miraculous indwelling manifestation. An example is the Ethiopian eunuch. (Acts 8:26-40.)

The scriptures clearly teach the free moral agency of man and they do not teach the doctrines of total depravity, unlimited election, limited atonement, irresistible grace, or perseverance of the saints. Therefore, the Calvinistic doctrine of the direct operation of the Holy Spirit on an elect person to effect his salvation, and the continual operation on that person to effect his sanctification, is without foundation in the scriptures. However, it is beyond the scope of this study to refute the Calvinistic theories.

Prominent Views in the Restoration Movement

Most all commentators are agreed on the fact of the indwelling of the Spirit. Restoration leaders comment in unison on this point, but they are reluctant to discuss how. They uniformly agree that he does not dwell miraculously but are divided as to whether he dwells personally or representatively.

Whiteside says in his comments on Rom. 8:9, "But the Spirit of God is the Holy Spirit. He dwells in the Christian; that is plainly affirmed. And I dare not deny what paul here affirms." [35]

Lard comments as follows:

The Holy Spirit dwells in the regenerate heart. This I set down as a fact too clearly taught in holy Writ to be questioned.

But how does Christ dwell in Christians; for the **though** of the clause concedes the fact. The inquiry, be it noticed, respects the mode only, of the dwelling. Accordingly I reply, he dwells not in person, but representatively. He dwells in Christians by his Spirit. Paul tells the disciples in Ephesus that they were built together for a dwelling-place of God in or by the Spirit. Now as God dwelt in them, so Christ dwells in us. The Spirit dwells literally in us, Christ, by the Spirit. The mode of this dwelling we do not affect to understand. It is inexplicable. The fact of it we accept, but venture on no explanations.[36]

Personal Indwelling of the Spirit

The author of the Gospel Advocate Annual argues strongly for the personal indwelling of the Holy Spirit in Christians.

The original word for the expression "if so be that" (*eiper*) means, according to Arndt-Gingrich, **if indeed, if after all, since**; and the passage is translated by Moffatt in these words: "But you are not in the flesh, you are in the Spirit, since the Spirit of God dwells within you." The personal indwelling of the Holy Spirit is not only clearly taught in the New Testament (I Cor. 6:19, 20); it is essential if one is to be in favor with God (Acts 2:38, 39; 5:32; Eph. 3:14-19).

We learn from Eph. 3:14ff that Christ dwells in the hearts of Christians by faith, as a result of the preparation made by the Spirit, which is another way of saying that they have been renewed or made new creatures (2 Cor. 5:17; Tit. 3:5); or, to change the figure somewhat, God's people today are made "into a holy temple in the Lord; in whom ye are also builded together for a habitation of God in the Spirit." (See Eph. 2:19-22.) [37]

In another place he says,

Hall L. Calhoun notes that the indwelling of the Holy Spirit in a Christian is taught as plainly as any other truth found in the Bible. This text makes it clear that the Spirit does dwell in our bodies. But this is not to be understood in any miraculous or mysterious sense. It simply means that our bodies, along with our whole being, have been redeemed by Christ, that they belong to him, and that they are to be used as the Spirit who has taken up his abode in them directs. This, again, does not mean that the Spirit acts independently of his word in dealing with our bodies, but that he gives instruction through his revealed will regarding the way we should live. (Cf. Rom. 8:2, 14.) The body is made a suitable dwelling place for the Spirit when one obeys the gospel. (See Acts 2:36-39; 5:32; Gal. 3:14.) [38]

And again the Annual states,

From these two passages we learn that the Spirit of Christ is the Holy Spirit. So when the Holy Spirit came to the apostles, the Spirit of Christ came and the promise of Christ to come unto them was fulfilled. The Father and the Son dwell in us representatively. Paul tells us that "we are builded together for a habitation of God in the Spirit." (Eph. 2:22.) From this we learn that God the Father dwells in us in the representative of the Holy Spirit and our text shows that Jesus dwells in us in the representative of the Holy Spirit. So the first and second persons of the Godhead do not dwell in us personally, but they dwell in us representatively in the person of the Holy Spirit, the third person of the Godhead. Christ in all his people [sic]. Paul says, "But if any man hath not the Spirit of Christ, he is none of his." (Rom. 8:9b.) From this we learn that if the Spirit of Christ which is the Holy Spirit does not dwell in us we do not belong to Christ. Hence, the Spirit of Christ, or Holy Spirit, dwells in all who belong to Christ by right of redemption. [39]

As arguments to prove the personal indwelling of the spirit, the *Annual* sets forth the following:

There are those who think that since the Holy Spirit is a person he cannot dwell in more than one person at a time, and give this as proof that the Holy Spirit does not personally dwell in Christians today. But Jesus promised that the Holy Spirit whom he would send would dwell in the apostles. This is proof that the Holy Spirit, though a person, can dwell in more than one human being at a time. [40]

Representative Indwelling of Spirit by Word

In this author's opinion, the most predominant view of Restoration leaders is that the Spirit dwells representatively in Christians by the medium of the word. Perhaps the reason for this is that so much emphasis has been placed on the operation of the Spirit through the word in conversion of sinners that it has been assumed that he operates the same way in sanctification of saints.

The view of the indwelling of the Spirit by means of the word is ably expressed by Brother Boles. After pointing to several passages that teach that God and Christ dwell in Christians he then observes,

How does God and Christ dwell in us? This question is answered with the following Scripture:

"Whosoever goeth onward and abideth not in the teaching of Christ, hath not God: he that abideth in the teaching, the same hath both the Father and The Son." (2 John 9.) Neither God nor Christ dwells personally in us. God is in his heavens and Christ is at the right hand of God; Christ has ascended back to the Father, so he does not dwell in us in person. He dwells in us through his representative. The Holy Spirit represents God and Christ on the earth. When the Holy Spirit dwells in Christians, God and Christ dwell in them. The Holy Spirit dwells in Christians. "Know ye not that ye are a temple of God, and that the Spirit of god dwelleth in you? If any man destroyeth the temple of God, him shall God destroy; for the temple of God is holy, and such are ye." (I Cor. 3:16, 17.) So God dwells in Christians through the Holy Spirit. "Or think ye that the scripture speaketh in vain? Doth the spirit which he made to dwell in us long unto envying?" (James 4:5.) As God and Christ dwell in us through the Holy Spirit, so the Holy Spirit dwells in us through his agent, the word of truth. "My little children, of whom I am again in travail until Christ be formed in you." (Gal. 4:19.) For Christ to be "formed" in us is the development of the spiritual life; this life is developed by the Holy Spirit through his agency, the word of God. All growth of the regenerated life and character conforms to the laws of the Holy Spirit in all of his workings. When the word of Christ dwells in Christians, the Holy Spirit dwells in them. The Holy Spirit and the word of God are inseparable; the word of God is the word of the Holy Spirit. "Let the word of Christ dwell in you richly" (Col. 3:16) is the way for Christ to dwell in us; it is the way for the Holy Spirit to dwell in us....

There is a sense in which the Holy Spirit in the "ordinary measure" dwelt with all Christians; in this measure he dwells with Christians today. In this sense all of the references to the indwelling of the Spirit in Christians find their application. The more faithful a Christian is the more of the Spirit of Christ he has; the more consecrated Christians are the richer and fuller are the blessings of the Holy Spirit. [41]

While Brother Boles distinguishes between the Holy Spirit as the agent and the word as the instrument, for all practical purposes, he eliminates this by making the action of the Spirit identical to that of the word so that no other operation of the Spirit is recognized. Note his statements:

> A further distinction should be made between the word of God and the indwelling of the Holy Spirit. The word of God, the New Testament, the word of truth, is the instrument which the Holy Spirit employs. We should not mistake the **instrument** for the **agent**; it would be folly to make no distinction between the instrument of a man that he may use in his work and the man himself. Perhaps some have made the gross error in concluding that the indwelling of the Holy Spirit is nothing more than the presence of the word of God in the mind or memory of the Christian. It may be that we cannot tell the difference so that others may see or understand it; however, there is a difference between our words and our spirits. In like manner there is a difference in the Holy Spirit and the words of the Holy Spirit. [42]

> The Holy Spirit and the word of God are inseparable and also identical in their action on the hearts of men. Whatever is affirmed of the Spirit in the redemption of man is also affirmed of the word of God. Some of the important actions of the Holy Spirit are here listed with scriptural reference showing that the same actions are affirmed of the word of God. The scriptural references for the action of the Holy Spirit are placed in the first column and those of the word of God in the third column, with the action placed in the middle column.

Holy Spirit	Action	Word of God
Gen. 1:2;	In creation	Heb. 1:3;
Job 33:4		II Pet. 3:5
2 Cor. 3:6	Gives life	James 1:18
John 3:8	Born of	I Pet. 1:23-25

Holy Spirit	Action	Word of God
Tit. 3:5	Salvation	James 1:21
I Cor. 6:11;	Sanctification	John 17:17
2 Thess. 2:13		
Rom. 8:11	Dwells in	Col. 3:16
I John 5:7	Spirit is truth	John 17:17
Rom. 15:13	Power of	Heb. 1:3

Whatever is declared of the Holy Spirit is also declared of the word of God. [43]

The same argument for the Spirit operating through the word is made by Brother C. R. Nichol. [44]

Still another Restoration author argues for the Spirit indwelling through the medium of the word in much the same way.

If God (the first member of the Godhead) can dwell in his children and in his church in this century without doing so miraculously, and if Christ (the second member of the Godhead) can dwell in his followers today without doing so miraculously (Christ dwells in his followers through faith—Eph. 3:17), and if Satan can dwell in persons without doing so miraculously, then why cannot the Holy Spirit (the third member of the Godhead) dwell in God's children today without doing so miraculously, but through the medium of Christ's word? The Spirit's dwelling in the heart of a child of God in this century does not give that person a "mysterious" feeling! [45]

The brethren who believe in representative indwelling by means of the word often criticize those holding the view of the actual indwelling of the Holy Spirit because they say the Holy Spirit dwells in Christians "personally". They contend the scriptures nowhere use the word "personally". I would respond by saying "Show me the verse that says 'representatively' and I will show the verse that says 'personally'."

Neither of these words are in scripture and none of us should engage in the practice of putting words in the mouth of the Holy Spirit which he did not use.

Conclusion on the Indwelling of the Spirit

The scriptures clearly teach that the indwelling of the Spirit is not merely representatively by the word "only". It is more than the mere knowledge that one has of the word. This is made clear by an examination of the following passages:

1. In Acts 2:38 the promise of the gift of the Holy Spirit is made to those after they had heard, believed, repented, and been baptized. Therefore, they received much of the word or message of the gospel before they could receive the Holy Spirit. It.is thus clear that the gift of the Holy Spirit was to be something other than the gift or the hearing of the word.

2. In Acts 5:32, the Holy Spirit was given to those who obeyed God. However, to obey Him, they had to have heard the word and possessed it in their lives before obedience would be possible. Therefore, the giving of the Holy Spirit, which came after their obedience, must be something more than the possession of the word.

3. In Galatians 4:6 the Holy Spirit was sent into the hearts of the Christians because they were sons. However, in order to become sons, they had to have heard the word. Therefore, since the Holy Spirit was sent to them after they became sons, the possession of the Holy Spirit must be something different from the possession of the word.

4. In Ephesians 1:13, Paul affirms that the Ephesians had heard the word of truth, the gospel of their salvation. Then they were sealed with the Holy Spirit. Therefore, again the possession of the Holy Spirit is something different from possession of the word because they had already possessed

the word before they possessed the Holy Spirit. From the above passages it is clear that the process or order involved is: (1) receive the word; (2) obey the word; (3) become sons; and (4) receive the Holy Spirit. Therefore, the indwelling of the Holy Spirit is separate and distinct from the indwelling of the word.

5. In Psalms 51:11 David prayed to God not to take the Holy Spirit from him. Certainly David was not expecting God to take the law of Moses from him or blot out all he knew of the law of Moses from his mind. This passage clearly shows that the possession of the Holy Spirit was different from the possession of the word, or knowledge of the law.

6. John 14:17 affirms that the world cannot receive the Holy Spirit. However, the world must receive the word of God in order to hear, believe, repent, confess and be baptized and be translated out of the kingdom of the world into the kingdom of God's dear Son. Therefore, it is clear that the indwelling of the Holy Spirit is distinct from and something more than the dwelling of the word of God in one's heart.

7. The sum of all of this evidence is that the scriptures clearly teach that both the word of God and the Holy Spirit dwell in the Christian. If God had wanted to say that the Holy Spirit dwells in the Christian representatively by the word, the Greek words were available to say so. What God did say is that the word should dwell in the Christian and that the Holy Spirit dwells in the Christian. Therefore, his word clearly teaches that both the word and the Holy Spirit dwell in the Christian.

8. It is quite possible for one to have a great possession of the word, but have no possession of the Spirit. Two examples are sufficient. A certain liberal college professor has a knowledge of the New Testament that surpasses most Christians and even gospel preachers. Yet he does not believe the spiritual

message of the New Testament, and therefore does not have the Holy Spirit. Again, an elder of the Lord's church well versed in the scripture, stood before the Lord's Supper one day, threw his Bible on the table upon which the communion was set, and said, "There's nothing to it" and walked out of the building. This man did not possess any less of the knowledge of the word of God, but certainly as he continued in his impenitent state there can be no doubt that the Spirit of God no longer dwelt in him.

The scriptures indicate as plainly as words can that the indwelling of the Holy Spirit is a special presence or accompaniment of the Spirit with the child of God. It is far more than the omnipresence of the Holy Spirit. The scriptures mean by the indwelling of the Holy Spirit, that the Spirit is present with the Christian in a special unique way.

We must accept what the scriptures say, that the Spirit dwells in us. God has not chosen to reveal to us exactly how the Spirit dwells in us. We do not understand how the human spirit dwells in us, but we accept it. Even so, we may not comprehend how the Holy Spirit dwells in us, but we must accept that he does.

The Work of the Indwelling Holy Spirit

The Scriptures teach that the Holy Spirit dwells in the Christian, helping us with our infirmities and aiding us in sanctification without violating our free moral agency. Among the works or deeds of the Holy Spirit, one of the most important is leading the sanctified. The following passages state this function.

Rom. 8:14—"For as many as are led by the Spirit of God, these are sons of God."
Gal. 5:18—"But if ye are led by the Spirit, ye are not under the law."

The Leading of the Spirit

Leading by word. Since the leading thought of the Restoration leaders has been that the Holy Spirit dwells in Christians representatively by means of the word, the conclusion has naturally followed that the Holy Spirit leads only by means of the word. This view is stated by Brother Hobbs as follows:

> Yes, we believe in the Spirit. We believe that he operates today through the Spirit-inspired word. The word is the sword of the Spirit, Eph. 6:17. There is a sense in which God, Christ, and the Spirit all dwell in Christians . . .he says: "Let the word of Christ dwell in you richly . . ." Col. 3:16.

> We must be led by the teaching of the Spirit in becoming a Christian and in living the Christian life, Rom. 8:14. If we permit the Spirit-inspired word of Christ to dwell in us richly, then we will bear the fruit of the Spirit, Gal. 5:22, 23.[48]

Brother Boles, one of the greatest leaders of the Restoration, strongly states his conviction in these words,

> So the Holy Spirit leads people by speaking to them. He speaks to people in the New Testament. When people follow the New Testament, they are following the Holy Spirit. When they do what the Holy Spirit teaches, they are being led by the Holy Spirit...

> To follow the New Testament is to follow the Holy Spirit; to do what the Holy Spirit teaches one to do is to do what the New Testament requires. To be guided by the New Testament is to be guided by the Holy Spirit. The Holy Spirit leads all the same way; he does not lead one man into one church and another into another church; he leads all into the church of our Lord. The Holy Spirit does not lead one Christian one way and lead another still another way. What

the New Testament says to one it says to everyone. What the Holy Spirit says to one he says to everyone in that condition. Hence, all Christians are led the same way; they are led to wear the same name, to worship the same way, and to develop into the likeness of Christ. All should yield to the simple teachings of the New Testament, for in doing so they are led by the Holy Spirit.[49]

Another respected leader in the brotherhood, Brother Whiteside, in his commentary on Romans 8:14 advocates the same concept.

> Nothing is here said as to how the Spirit leads people; but as Paul is still developing his theme that the gospel is God's power to save, it is certain that the Spirit leads through the power of the gospel. The gospel was revealed by the Spirit. In that revelation the Spirit tells us how to live, and sets motives before us to induce us to follow his directions. But if the Spirit, independent of the gospel, leads people to become children of God, then the gospel is not God's power to save. We are sure Paul did not make an assertion about the Holy Spirit that contradicted his theme and his argument.[50]

Leading in addition to word. However, dissenting and modifying voices also have been heard on this subject. Brother McGarvey and Brother Lard speak as one on the leading of the Spirit.

> The Spirit leads both externally and internally. Externally, the Spirit supplies the gospel truth as set forth in the New Testament, and the rules and precepts therein found are for the instruction and guidance of God's children. Internally, the Spirit aids by ministering strength and comfort to the disciple in his effort to conform to the revealed truth and will of God. [51]

> But what kind of "leading" is here meant—an occult, internal, inexplicable leading, or an external, explicable one by the truth? Before replying, let us ask, who are led?

Certainly not the unconverted, but christians. In those led, then, the Holy Spirit already dwells. What kind of leading then is it? I answer, both internal and external. To whatever extent the Holy Spirit by its indwelling strengthens the human spirit, to enable it to control the flesh, to that extent the leading is internal. To whatever extent the motives of the gospel, when brought to bear on the mind in the written word, enlighten and strengthen it, and so enable it to keep the body in subjection, to that extent the leading is external. The leading, then, consists of the whole of the influences of every kind, spent by the Holy Spirit on the human spirit, in enabling it to keep the body under. More definitively than this it would not be wise to attempt to speak. [52]

In addition to these early Restoration leaders, a recent author in the *Gospel Advocate Annual* gave these comments on the leading of the Spirit.

Christians are taught to ask for guidance for all their needs; and as certain as God through the Spirit answers their prayers, just that certain are they being led by the Spirit. (See Phil. 4:6, 7; Heb. 13:5, 6; 4:14-16; Rom. 8:26, 27.)

The leading of the Spirit, therefore, consists of all the influences of every kind which he brings to bear upon our spirits, and which enable us to keep the body under control, or, which is the same thing, to live the kind of life which is acceptable to God. "So then, my beloved, even as ye have always obeyed, not as in my presence only, but now much more in my absence, work out your own salvation with fear and trembling; **for it is God who worketh in you both to will and to work, for his good pleasure.**" (Phil. 2:12, 13.) Of one thing we may be certain, the Holy Spirit never leads anyone to do anything short of, more than, or different from what is clearly taught in the word, which is the "sword of the Spirit."...

All through this section of our lesson Paul is setting forth the proof that we are children of God, if we are led by the Spirit. It has already been pointed out that the Spirit leads people both by the teaching of the word, and through God's providential care. [53]

Other strong voices in support of both internal and external leading of the Holy Spirit are those of Brother Lipscomb and Brother Shepherd. They conclude also that the leading consists of the whole of the influences of every kind exercised by the Holy Spirit on the Human Spirit, enabling it to keep the body under. [54]

Conclusion. It is the conclusion of this author that although the Holy Spirit never leads one in any way contrary to the word or in a way contrary to free moral agency, that nevertheless, the Spirit leads and aids the Christian in his efforts to righteousness. It is a further conclusion that gospel preachers and teachers have been driven to the extreme view that the Spirit leads only through the word because of arguments in debates with religious groups which stress the direct operation of the Holy Spirit. Thus, because no clear distinction was made between the operation of the Spirit in conversion on the sinner who has not the Spirit and the operation of the Spirit in sanctification of the saint who has received the Spirit, brethren have taken the easy-to-explain position that the Holy Spirit leads only through the word.

The fact that one does not know exactly how the Spirit might lead Christians internally, does not take away from the comforting thought that the Spirit does help. Christians are taught to pray for deliverance from temptation. This must mean help in addition to the word. The disciples asked for increased faith. This must be in addition to that which comes through study of the word. Faith may be increased by providential acts of God, answered prayer, and in other ways. The early Christians prayed for boldness to speak the word. (Acts 4:23-32.) This was certainly a request for help in addition to the word itself.

Thus, there are many ways the Spirit might lead us without giving us additional inspiration or violating free moral agency. Even concerning the word in overcoming temptation, the spirit could stimulate our minds so we remember the right scriptures at the right time. This could also be true with preaching and personal work. We often pray that we may say and do the right things at the right time so our work will be effective. The Holy Spirit may work both providentially and through the word in these cases. Therefore, one does not have to understand every way the Holy Spirit might lead on in order to pray for guidance and take comfort in the assurance that he does lead Christians.

The Witness and Intercession of the Spirit

In addition to the work of leading, Romans eight also introduces the work of the Holy Spirit as a witness and in prayer.

> Rom. 8:16, 17—"The Spirit himself beareth witness with our spirit, that we are children of God: and if children, then heirs; heirs of God, and joint-heirs with Christ; if so be that we suffer with him, that we may be also glorified with him."

> Rom. 8:26, 27—"And in like manner the Spirit also helpeth our infirmity: for we know not how to pray as we ought; but the Spirit himself maketh intercession for us with groanings which cannot be uttered; and he that searcheth the hearts knoweth what is the mind of the Spirit, because he maketh intercession for the saints according to the will of God."

Discussion. As on the preceding points, there are two main viewpoints: one, the operation of the Spirit only through the word; two, the operation of the indwelling Spirit in accordance with the word. Lengthy and numerous quotations are not now necessary since these two views have been thoroughly set forth.

The view expressed by Brother Boles,[55] Whiteside,[56] and others is that the witnessing is done by the human spirit testifying what it has done and the Holy Spirit testifying what must be done. Thus, when they agree they bear witness that the obedient one is a child of God. Likewise concerning prayer, Brother Boles argues that the Spirit helps a Christian to pray by teaching how to pray and for what.

On the other hand, Brother Lard, Brother McGarvey, and others contend that the witness of the Spirit involves an internal assurance to the Christian that he is following a course of obedience. Also on prayer, they comment that the Spirit expresses one's unexpressable thoughts, one's needs that are desired but not understood. [57]

Conclusion. It is the conclusion of this researcher that the Holy Spirit bears witness and helps in prayer both through the word and in spiritual, providential ways that may not be clear to us. Yet, even though not clear, Christians are still comforted, encouraged and blessed by the indwelling gift and operation of the Spirit. The following points may help to understand this aspect of the work of the Holy Spirit.

1. The Christian age is clearly the age or economy of the Holy Spirit. Christ sent the Spirit to guide and be with Christians.

2. There are many promises of blessings and services to be rendered to the Christian. It is not unreasonable to assume that the indwelling Holy Spirit operates in some measure in fulfilling and directing these promises and services.

3. Romans 8:26 affirms that the Spirit helps our infirmities and especially makes supplication or intercession on our behalf.

4. Hebrews 1:14 promises that angels minister in behalf of Christians. Perhaps the Holy Spirit directs the ministry of the angels in our behalf. This ministry may include providential protection from danger, or providential assistance in accomplishing good works.

5. Matthew 6:33 promises that material needs will be added to those who seek first the kingdom and righteousness. The Holy Spirit may well aid us by fulfilling this promise.

6. Romans 8:28 promises that all things will work together for good for those who love the Lord, and are called according to His calling. Certainly the Holy Spirit is the chief medium of accomplishing this.

7. I Corinthians 10:13 promises that there may be a way of escape from every temptation and indeed the Spirit could help us to find this way of escape when we truly want to without in any way interfering with our free moral agency.

8. Many passages promise the answers to prayer and the Spirit can help us repeatedly by answering our prayers, such as leading us away from temptation.

9. James 1:5-8 promises that if we lack wisdom, we may ask of God and He will give it to us. The Spirit certainly may be involved in granting us wisdom. One of the greatest weaknesses and dangers of the theory of the Spirit dwelling in us representatively is that it denies the operation of the Spirit to lead us in any practical way. We have a common practice in our church business meetings of beginning them with a prayer for wisdom to make the right decisions, but if the Spirit leads in no way except through the word, we would do better to cease praying and to spend that time reading the word. Certainly no one who believes the scriptures and the indwelling of the Holy Spirit, believes that the Spirit reveals any new truth to us or brings to our mind any scripture we have not studied. However, it is perfectly consistent with God's word and free moral agency for the Holy Spirit to help us to arrange our thoughts and to bring to our remembrance information that will be of help to us in making the right decision in the right situation.

10. Colossians 4:6 urges that our speech always be with grace seasoned with salt. I try to make it a practice to always pray before I preach that the Lord will help me to say the right words in the right way to be the most effective in reaching

and teaching people. I do not expect God to give me any new revelation. However, I do firmly believe that God, by his Spirit or his angels or by some means, will answer that prayer and help me to proclaim God's word effectively. Any mistakes I make, however, will not be the fault of the Holy Spirit but my failure to subdue myself completely to the Holy Spirit.

Since the scriptures do not reveal to us exactly how the Holy Spirit indwells the Christian, there should be no reason for strife, or division among us over the question of how the Holy Spirit dwells in the Christian so long as we all believe and teach that the Holy Spirit does dwell in faithful and obedient children of God. However, there are some theories among us which greatly misinterpret scriptures in order to lessen their affirmation concerning the indwelling of the Holy Spirit. Other theories among us come very close to denying the affirmation of the scriptures that the Holy Spirit helps our infirmities and that our prayers for wisdom will be answered. We must be careful not to accept nullifying theories, but rather we must rejoice that the Spirit dwells in us and thereby cry "Abba Father."

FOOTNOTES

1 Phillip Schaff, *History of the Christian Church* (Grand Rapids: Wm. B. Eerdmans Publishing Co., 1910), I, 464.

2 George P. Fisher, *History of the Christian Church* (New York: Charles Scribner's Sons, 1915), p. 81.

3 J. L. Neve, *A History of Christian Thought* (Philadelphia: The Muhlenberg Press, 1946), I, 119.

4 *Ibid.,* p. 119.

5 *Ibid.,* p. 266.

6 *Ibid.,* p. 283.

7 *Loc. cit.,* Calvin's *Institutes* IV, pp. 16, 19.

8 Earl West, *The Search for the Ancient Order* (Nashville: Gospel Advocate Co., 1949), I, p. 23.

9 N. B. Hardeman and Ben M. Bogard, *Hardeman-Bogard Debate* (Nashville: Gospel Advocate Co., 1942), p. 7.

10 H. Leo Boles, *The Holy Spirit—His Personality, Nature, Works* (Nashville: Gospel Advocate Co., 1942), p. 192.

11 Robert Young, *Analytical Concordance to the Bible* (New York: Funk & Wagnalls Co., 22nd Am. Ed.), Index-Lexicon, p. 86.

12 *Analytical Greek Lexicon* (Grand Rapids: Zondervan Publishing House, 1972), p. 124.

13 W. E. Vine, *An Expository Dictionary of New Testament Words* (Westwood: Fleming H. Revell Company), p. 201.

14 Alfred Marshall, *The Interlinear Greek-English New Testament with The Nestle Greek Text* (London: Samuel Bagster and Sons Limited, 2nd Ed., 1970), p. 430.

15 Paul Southern, *The Person and Work of the Holy Spirit* (Nashville: World Vision Publishing Co., 5tn Ed.), p. 4.

16 *Ibid.,* p. 5.

17 *Loc. cit.*

18 *Ibid.,* p. 6.

19 *Ibid.,* p. 7.

20 Boles, *op. cit.,* p. 46.

21 E. W. Bullinger, *The Giver and his Gifts* (London: Eyre and Spottiswoode, 1905), pp. 26-41, 89. This work lists and discusses all 388 occurrences of *pneuma* in the Greek New Testament.

22 Young, *op. cit.,* p. 70; Matt. 3:11; Mark 1:8; Luke 3:16; John 1:33; Acts 1:5; 11:16.

23 Boles, *op. cit.,* pp. 151-153.

24 Edd Holt, Unpublished Sermon on the Holy Spirit.

25 James Strong, *The Exhaustive Concordance of the Bible* (Nashville: Abingdon-Cokesbury Press, 1890), p. 969.

26 Joseph H. Thayer, *A Greek-English Lexicon of the New Testament* (New York: American Book Company, 1889), p. 132.

27 *Ibid.,* p. 402.

28 Ashley S. Johnson, *The Holy Spirit and the Human Mind* (Dallas: Eugene S. Smith Publisher, 1950), p. 48.

29 *The Englishman's Greek Concordance of the New Testament* (London: Samuel Bagster and Sons, 1903), pp. 629, 630.

30 *The Analytical Greek Lexicon*, pp. 324, 328.

31 W. E. Vine, *An Expository Dictionary of New Testament Words* (Westwood, N. J.: Fleming H. Revell Company, 1962), pp. 344-345.

32 *Ibid.,* p. 345.

33 *Loc. cit.*

34 Gerhard F. Kittel, *Theological Dictionary of the New Testament* (Grand Rapids: Wm. B. Eerdmans Publishing Company, 1967), Vol. V, p. 135.

35 R. L. Whiteside, *Paul's Letter to the Saints at Rome* (Clifton, Texas: Nichol Publishing Co., 2nd Ed., 1948), p. 173.

36 Moses E. Lard, *Paul's Letter to Romans* (Delight, Arkansas: Gospel Light Publishing Company, 1875), pp. 257, 258.

37 *Teacher's Annual Lesson Commentary, 1963* (Nashville: Gospel Advocate Company, 1962), XLII, p. 111.

38 *Ibid.,* XL, 231.

39 *Ibid.,* XXXVI, 202.

FOOTNOTES

40 *Ibid.,* XXXVI, 203.
41 Boles, *op. cit.,* pp. 207-209.
42 *Ibid.,* pp. 204, 205.
43 *Ibid.,* pp. 191-192.
44 C. R. Nichol, *Nichol's Pocket Bible Encyclopedia* (Clifton, Texas: The Nichol Publishing Co., 1949), p. 140.
45 Eris B. Benson, *The Bible Teaches* (Montgomery: Eris B. Benson, Publisher, 1955), p. 78.
48 A. G. Hobbs, Jr., *Holy Spirit Baptism* (Ft. Worth: A. G. Hobbs, Jr. Publisher, 1953), pp. 19, 20.
49 Boles, *op. cit.,* pp. 238, 241.
50 Whiteside, *op. cit.,* p. 177.
51 J. W. McGarvey, *Thessalonians, Corinthians, Galatians and Romans* (Cincinnati: The Standard Publishing Company, 1916), p. 361.
52 Lard, *op. cit.,* p. 264.
53 *Teacher's Annual Lesson Commentary,* XL, pp. 161, 162.
54 *Ibid.,* XLII, 112.
55 Boles, *op. cit.,* pp. 217, 256.
56 Whiteside, *op. cit.,* p. 178.
57 Lard, *op. cit.,* pp. 266, 276.

BIBLIOGRAPHY

Analytical Greek Lexicon. Grand Rapids: Zondervan Publishing House, 1973. 444 pp.

Bales, James D. *The Holy Spirit and The Christian*. Shreveport, Louisiana: Gussie Lambert Publications, 1966. 147 pp.

Barclay, William. *The Letter to the Romans*. Philadelphia: The Westminster Press, 1957. 244 pp.

Benson, Eris B. *The Bible Teaches*. Montgomery: Eris B. Benson, Publisher, 1955. 92 pp.

Boles, H. Leo. *The Holy Spirit, His Personality, Nature, Works*. Nashville: Gospel Advocate Company, 1942. 306 pp.

Camp, Franklin. *The Work of the Holy Spirit in Redemption*. Birmingham: Roberts & Son, 1974. 274 pp.

Challen, James. *A Symposium on the Holy Spirit*. (First published by John Burns, 1879; reprinted by College Press, Joplin, Missouri, 1966). 107 pp.

Englishman's Greek Concordance. Grand Rapids: Zondervan Publishing House, 1971. 1020 pp.

Fisher, George P. *History of the Christian Church*. New York: Charles Scribner's Sons, 1915. 729 pp.

Hardeman, N. B. and Ben M. Bogard. *Hardeman-Bogard Debate*. Nashville: Gospel Advocate Company, 1938. 320 pp.

Hervey, A. C. and J. Bramby. *The Acts of the Apostles, The Epistle of Paul to the Romans*, Vol. XVIII of *The Pulpit Commentary*, ed. by H. D. M. Spence and Joseph S. Exell. Grand Rapids: Wm. B. Eerdmans Publishing Co., 1950. 838 pp.

Hobbs, A. G., Jr. *Holy Spirit Baptism.* Fort Worth: A. G. Hobbs, Publisher, 1953. 20 pp.

Holt, Edd. Unpublished Sermon on the Holy Spirit.

Jividen, Jimmy. *Glossolalia–From God or Man?* Fort Worth: Star Bible Publications, 1971. 196 pp.

        Indwelling of the Holy Spirit. Fort Worth: Star Bible Publications, no publication date. 14 pp.

Johnson, Ashley. *Holy Spirit and the Human Mind.* Dallas: Eugene S. Smith, Publisher, 1950. 290 pp.

Lanier, Roy H., Sr. *The Gift of the Holy Spirit,* Arts. I-V. Austin: Firm Foundation, 11-20-73, 11-27-73, 12-4-73, 12-11-73, 12-18-73. 6 pp.

Lard, Moses E. *Commentary on Paul's Letter to Romans.* Delight, Arkansas: Gospel Light Publishing Company, 1875. 485 pp.

McGarvey, J. W. and Phillip Y. Pendleton. *Thessalonians, Corinthians, Galatians, and Romans.* Cincinnati: The Standard Publishing Company, 1916. 555 pp.

Macknight, James. *A New Translation from the Original Greek of all the Apostical Epistles with A Commentary.* Grand Rapids: Baker Book House, 1949. 776 pp.

Marshall, Alfred. *The Interlinear Greek-English New Testament.* London: Samuel Bagster and Sons, Ltd., 1960. 1027 pp.

Neve, J. L. *A History of Christian Thought.* Philadelphia: Muhlenberg Press, 1946. 2 vols.

Nichol, C. R. and J. W. Denton. *Nichol's Pocket Bible Encyclopedia.* Clifton, Texas: Mrs. C. R. Nichol, Publisher, 1949. 219 pp.

Nichols, Gus and C. G. Weaver. *Nichols-Weaver Debate.* Nashville: Gospel Advocate Company, 1944. 221 pp.

Porter, W. Curtis and Glenn V. Tingley. *Porter-Tingley Debate.* Murfreesboro: George DeHoff, 1947. 275 pp.

Rogers, Richard. *A Study of The Holy Spirit of God.* Lubbock, Texas: World Missions Publishing Company, 1968. 85 pp.

Sanday, W. and A. C. Headlam. *The Epistle to the Romans,* a vol. of *The International Critical Commentary,* ed. by Charles Briggs, Samuel Driver and Alfred Plummer. New York: Charles Scribner's Sons, 1906. 450 pp.

Schaff, Phillip. *History of the Christian Church.* Grand Rapids: Wm. B. Eerdmans Publishing Company, 1910. 8 vols.

Southern, Paul. *The Person and Work of the Holy Spirit.* Nashville: World Vision Publishing Company, no date. 13 pp.

Strong, James. *The Exhaustive Concordance of the Bible.* Nashville: Abingdon-Cokesbury Press, 1890. 1340 pp.

Teacher's Annual Lesson Commentary on Bible School Lessons. Nashville: Gospel Advocate Company. 42 vols.

Thayer, Joseph Henry. *Greek-Lexicon of the New Testament.* Grand Rapids: Zondervan Publishing House, 1962. 726 pp.

Vine, W. E. *An Expository Dictionary of New Testament Words.* Westwood: Fleming H. Revell Company, 1962. 351 pp.

Wallace, Foy E., Jr. *The Mission and Medium of the Holy Spirit.* Nashville: Foy E. Wallace, Jr., Publications, 1967. 120 pp.

West, Earl Irvin. *The Search for the Ancient Order.* Nashville: Gospel Advocate Company, 1949. 358 pp.

Young, Robert. *Analytical Concordance to the Bible*. New York: Funk & Wagnalls, no date. 1251 pp.

Whiteside, Robertson L. *A New Commentary on Paul's Letter to the Saints at Rome*. Clifton, Texas: Mrs. C. R. Nichol, Publisher, 1948. 301 pp.

Woods, Guy N. *How the Holy Spirit Dwells in the Christian*. Shreveport: Lambert Book House, 1971. 24 pp.